WHAT DOES IT
FEEL LIKE

....to be a Child
With Autism?

By: Coretta Conant
Illustrated by: Travis Taylor

Dedication

To the Late Mr. & Mrs. James W. Anthony for all of your love and guidance.

My husband Greg and daughter April

For the children who have passed through my classroom you will always have a special place in my heart.

I remember years ago while riding my dad's school bus, there was a boy named David. He often would get into trouble while at school. Well, my dad knew this and tried hard to reach this young man. Dad would allow David to open the bus door as the school kids would enter the bus. I may not have known why dad did what he did at that time, but as I began my teaching career. I would soon find out. Dad had made a connection with David and that small act of allowing him to help on the school bus, could have been a turning point in David's life. While I don't know whatever happened to David. I do know that that sentiment was branded in my mind. I often think of its importance a great deal in my life.

I chose to become a teacher at first because it seemed like an easy choice. Prior to majoring in education, I was taking social work courses. This all changed when I began to work with children in the early '90's in Houston, Texas.

I am now in my 22nd year of teaching. I must say it has been one of the most rewarding experiences in my life. It has been my experience that I tend to work well with troubled youth or poor unkempt children. I remember vividly a kindergartner named Jeremiah. Jeremiah was a ball of fire, often dirty and smelled a little. But this kid grabbed my heart strings. He tried hard and wanted to please the teachers and the principal. He often came to school tattered and torn, but at the end of the year for our end of year celebration I went and purchased a nice outfit for him to wear. He wanted to be dressed like the assistant principal, Mr. M. who was always very well dressed. Needless to say by the end of the day his brand new shoes were scuffed and his shirt was untucked, but that did not matter at least for one day he got to dress up and look like his idol Mr. M.

Fast forward to the winter of 2021. That would be the day that a lightning bolt came into my classroom. His name was Noah. Before he came in I was warned that he had had some questionable behavioral outburst at his previous school. This child was a kindergartner with a paper trail that was a mile long. The description reads like this.

Elopement
Fails to listen
Jumping on tables
Turning over chairs
Yelling at teachers

The attendance clerk escorted him and his parents to my classroom. The father appeared young, quiet and he quickly removed himself from our conversation. I was told there was no contact with his biological mother. This student had a smile that warmed my heart immediately.

Upon meeting Noah, he appeared happy and eager to join my class. The first week he was there he fit right in with the class and had no issues so it seemed. Yet a week later the mask had come off. It was difficult at first for me to establish a pattern of behavior, but as the weeks passed, it would be revealed to me.

One Monday morning, Noah came into my classroom much earlier than the other students. He would appear angry, and would often tell me "I don't want to talk to you," so I would leave him alone. The room was quiet. As the bell rang, I noticed he would cover his ears with his hands. He yelled "Stop it, Stop it!" I quickly comforted him. He did not want that. He jerked away from me and then quickly eloped from the room. I would chart the number of times he would elope during the day. About three weeks of charting his elopement, while also building a bond with this little guy. Other characteristics began to emerge. I would ask myself where is this journey going to take me.

2.

I had a conversation with the school's diagnostician. I shared my experience with her. She suggested that I request to have the district psychologist come out and observe Noah. I contacted my principal and made the request to have the psychologist come out to the school. She quickly came out to the school the following week. We actually have known each other for years. This was not my first time asking for her assistance with a student who exhibited these types of characteristics. We spoke for a moment and then she proceeded to my classroom and observed him. The first observation showed him to be very calm, cordial and attentive. The next time she observed him, he was much more active and was acting out. He had to be escorted out of the classroom because he was jumping on the top of tables and desks, turning things over and leaving the class without permission. The district psychologist concluded that he was exhibiting classic signs of autism. She specifically termed it sensory overload.

As the school year progressed, his behavior did not diminish. It actually intensified. He quickly gained trust in me and wanted to be right next to me everyday all day. I was not sure why, but three days in, I saw with my own eyes. It was very clear this young man was being abused at home. The handprint on his face said it all. I asked what happened and he said "I can't talk about it". This was the genesis of the poem "What does it Feel Like"? You see, I, his teacher, was the person who saw all of the stares that he would get as he tried to walk from one end of the building to the other. I was the one who saw the other grown-ups whisper about him and looking right at him as they talked about him. One person even smirked, I would get so angry. I had to stifle myself. This is why I recited this poem at our end of year celebration. I wanted to be his voice. I wanted them, the teachers: aides and others to realize that their actions were seen, but the child was oblivious to it all.

Coretta Conant

3.

What does it feel like to be judged?

When no one knows your actions,

Aren't meant to be distractions.

When people look at you and make assumptions,

Yet do not know how your mind functions.

4.

What does it feel like when you are stared at?

Through the doors and down the halls,

Everywhere you walk,

Your presence attracts attention.

Can you feel when others gawk?

6.

What does it feel like to be talked about?

Teachers smile and welcome you,

A student in this space.

However, behind closed doors, they gossip and

They show their other face.

What does it feel like to be laughed at?

When your actions are impulsive,

And they do not understand.

All you can do is hang your head and hold it in your hands.

10.

What does it feel like to be hit?

Your parents don't understand that your brain is different from others.

They try to hide your bruises and scars,

They keep them under covers.

13.

What does it feel like to be hurt?

When Autism's misunderstood as a set of behavior problems,

The punishments and spankings come, unfortunately, often.

What does it feel like to be excluded?

It's time to go home,

But you're crouched in a corner,

Separate from them all.

Your teacher standing over you,

Her protection like a wall.

17.

What does it feel like to be hugged?

At the end of the day,

You are not alone,

You don't have to be scared.

You can rest assured,

Your help is here.

I, your teacher, really care.

18.

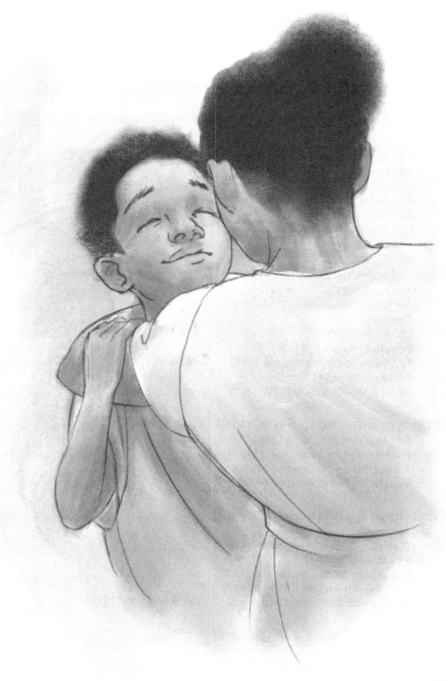

19.

Autismspeaks Resource Guide

Advocacy
-Advocacy, Legal & Financial [162]
-Advocates [299]
-Attorneys [202]
-Financial Planners [91]
-Legal & Financial [167]
-Parent Training [1, 319]

Autism Friendly Services
-After-school Programs [472]
-Art & Music Programs [250]
-Camps [384]
-Child Care [27]
-Equine Programs [117]
-Faith-Based Organizations [211]   -Haircuts [54]
-PPE Providers [4]
-Swim & Water Safety [110]

Employment & Post-Secondary Education
-Employment Supports [556]
-Post-Secondary Education [182]
-Transztttition Programs [395]
-Vocational Rehabilitation [473]

Evaluation & Diagnosis
-Autism Evaluation [918]
-Pediatricians - Developmental [90]
-Psychiatrists [164]
-Psychologists & Counselors [654]
-Specialized Autism Centers [439]
-Tele-health Evaluation Providers (Children and Adult) [105]

Health & Medical
-Allergist [15]
-Cardiologists [10]
-Dentists [255]
-Dermatologists [13]
-Endocrinologists [24]
-Gastroenterologists [32]
-Inpatient Treatment Care Centers [16]
-Internists [25]
-OBGYN [6]
-Orthodontists [36]
-Primary Care [70]
-Pulmonologists [23]
-Urologists [1]

Housing & Community Living
-Residential Programs [351]
-Transportation [126]

Multi-service providers
-Local Disability Organizations [139]
-Multi-service Providers [187]

Recreation & Community Activities
-Community Activities [458]
-Day Programs [425]
-Respite Care [347]
-Social Skills [1, 288]
-Virtual Programs (Social Skills, Social Groups, etc.) [314]

Safety
-First Responder Resources [33]

Schools
-Cyber School [40]
-Home School [33]
-Schools - Preschool [211]
-Schools - Private [298]
-Schools- Residential [34]

State Services & Entitlements
-Assistive Technology [151]
-Protection & Advocacy [88]
-Social Security Office Locator [4]
-Special Education Office [72]

Support
-Autism Speaks Communities [118]
-Support Groups [277]

Support Groups
-Adults [214]
-Family/Parent [366]
-Grandparents [63]
-Online Support Groups [55]
-Sibling [134]

Treatments & Therapies
-Applied Behavior Analysis (ABA) [2, 827]
-Early Start Denver Model [72]
-Floortime or DIR [122]
-Local Early Intervention Providers [799]
-Medicaid Waiver [281]
-Neurologists [69]
-Occupational Therapy [845]
-Physical Therapy [466]
-Pivotal Response Treatment (PRT) [105]
-Relationship Development Intervention (RDI) [77]
-Speech & Language Therapy [1, 118]
-State Developmental Disability Agency [65]
-State Early Intervention Office [175]
-TEACCH [26]
-Verbal Behavior [510]

https://www.autismspeaks.org/resource-guide

22.

ABOUT THE AUTHOR

Coretta Conant was reared in rural Louisiana in a place called Bermuda. She currently resides in Pearland, Texas. She is a graduate of the University Houston Clear Lake with a bachelor's degree in Interdisciplinary Sciences with emphasis on Early Childhood Education. She also has a master's degree in Curriculum and Instruction: Reading.

As an early childhood educator, I have taught a diverse range of students. In my 22 years the one that has had the most profound effect on me was those who had a diagnosis of Autism. They may see things differently, they may behave differently but overall they are still just kids.

This book was based on a poem that was inspired by past students of mine, from that poem came this book. I hope it sheds a little light on the plight a child with Autism may experience.

Teachers, students, families and individuals all around can start a real conversation about others who are perceived and treated differently.

23.